Helping Children See Jesus

ISBN: 978-1-64104-052-5

Sanctification

*New Testament Volume 21:
Romans Part 3*

Author: Marilyn P. Habecker
Illustrator: Frances H. Hertzler
Colorization courtesy of Good Life Ministries
Typesetting and Layout: Patricia Pope

© 2019 Bible Visuals International
PO Box 153, Akron, PA 17501-0153
Phone: (717) 859-1131
www.biblevisuals.org

All rights reserved. No part of this publication may be reproduced, stored in a retrieval system or transmitted in any form by any means, electronic, mechanical, photocopy, recording or otherwise, without the prior permission of the publisher, except as provided by USA copyright law.

RELATED ITEMS

To access related items (such as activities, memory verse posters and translated texts) please visit our web store at www.biblevisuals.org and enter 1021 at the top right of the web page. You may need to reduce the zoom setting to get the search box.

FREE TEXT DOWNLOAD

To obtain a FREE printable copy of the English teaching text (PDF format) under Product Format, please scroll down and select Extra–PDF Teacher Text Download. Then under Language select English before clicking the ADD TO CART button to place in your shopping cart. Other languages are available at an additional cost from the Language menu. When checking out, use coupon code XTACSV17 at checkout and click on Apply Coupon to receive the discount on the English text.

Lesson 1
SAMUEL IS SANCTIFIED

NOTE TO THE TEACHER

In the book of Romans, the Apostle Paul discusses condemnation, justification, and sanctification in this order. The believer in Christ is washed in the precious blood of the Lord Jesus Christ, justified and sanctified all at once. Every condemned sinner who places his trust in the Saviour is cleansed from sin, declared righteous, and set apart by God for God–all because of the death and resurrection of Christ the Lord. (See 1 Corinthians 6:11; Hebrews 10:10.) God's work in the trusting believer is perfect, complete, and immediate.

Sanctification has another aspect, however. Because the believer in Christ has been set apart, he is to be set apart increasingly in his daily life (1 Peter 1:16). All the New Testament exhortations concerning spiritual growth have to do with this progressive sanctification. The Christian is to set himself apart for God, growing continually in the image of His Son (Romans 8:29; Ephesians 4:14-15).

There is still another feature of sanctification. The believer will not be fully, perfectly set apart to God until he sees Christ and becomes as He is. (See 1 John 3:1-3.) This future sanctification awaits the Christian's complete glorification with a resurrection body. (See Ephesians 5:26-27; Jude 24-25.)

Some who have been set apart by Him do not live for Him. This, then, is a family matter. As disobedient children must be punished, so God disciplines His sanctified children who do not live to honor His Son.

Scripture to be studied: 1 Samuel 1:1–4:18; Romans 5:12–8:39

The *aim* of the lesson: To teach that those who truly believe in Christ are set apart by God for Himself.

What your students should *know*: God wants believers to serve Him.

What your students should *feel*: A desire to serve God.

What your students should *do*: Determine how they can serve the Lord this week.

Lesson outline (for the teacher's and students' notebooks):

1. Samuel, before birth, is set apart for the Lord (1 Samuel 1:1–2:11).
2. Though set apart for the Lord, Eli and his sons sin (1 Samuel 2:12-36).
3. God chooses Samuel for His service (1 Samuel 3:1-21).
4. Eli and his sons are judged by God (1 Samuel 4:1-18).

The verse to be memorized:

Ye are washed . . . ye are sanctified . . . ye are justified in the name of the Lord Jesus, and by the Spirit of our God.
(1 Corinthians 6:11b)

THE LESSON

In the first three chapters of Romans, we learn that God condemns the world. That is, He declares all are sinners; He proves that all are guilty; and He pronounces the eternal death sentence on all. This *condemnation* is bad news. However, the good news of Romans 4 and 5, is this: All who place their trust in God's Son, the Lord Jesus Christ, are justified. God, the righteous One, sees each believer in Christ. And because all God's righteousness is put to the believer's account, God announces him righteous. This is *justification*.

In the next section of Romans we learn that justified believers are also *sanctified*. That is the subject we will studying in this volume. Please write the following in your notebook:

Sanctification
Romans 5:21–8:39

"Sanctify" means *to set apart*. In English, the word often translated "sanctify" is translated at other times "holy," "hallowed," or "saint." *People* are spoken of as *saints* or *sanctified* or *holy*. *Things* and *places* are said to be *sanctified* or *holy*. When any one of these words (*saint, sanctify, hallow, holy*) is used, it means that the people or things are set apart for God.

God Himself–who condemns and justifies–is the One who sanctifies. (See Psalm 4:3.)

In this lesson we shall learn of four who were set apart–sanctified–by God. But each lived differently. Listen carefully!

1. SAMUEL, BEFORE BIRTH, IS SET APART FOR THE LORD
1 Samuel 1:1–2:11

Show Illustration #1

Hannah and her husband, Elkanah, had waited and hoped for a son for a long time. Year after year they went to God's house (a tent) to offer sacrifices to Him. There they prayed for a son. Finally Hannah promised God: "If You will hear me and give me a son, I shall give him to serve You all the days of his life."

Eli, a priest, sat by a post of the tent watching Hannah. Because he saw her lips move but did not hear any sound, he thought she was drunk–and told her so. Hannah explained, "No, I am not drunk. But I'm sad and am telling the Lord about my sadness." Hannah had her trust in the true God of Heaven, believing He could answer her prayer.

Eli knew, as Hannah did, that God, the all-powerful One, does answer prayer. So he told her, "Go in peace, and God give you what you have asked."

Within several months, God gave Hannah and Elkanah a baby boy. They named him Samuel meaning "Asked of God." A few years later Hannah kept her promise. She brought Samuel to live in the tent of God to serve Him there. Even though he was young, he had already learned to worship God. And that is what he did first at God's house.

Samuel knew it was a special honor to be set apart for the Lord's service. He would be expected to live a pure life and keep from doing anything that would dishonor and displease the Lord. Samuel obeyed Eli, the priest, doing all he was told to do. Surely his obedience pleased the Lord.

2. THOUGH SET APART FOR THE LORD, ELI AND HIS SONS SIN
1 Samuel 2:12-36

But God was not pleased with Eli's two sons, Hophni and Phinehas. They, like their father, were priests. Priests were set apart for special service to God. They were to be holy, obedient to God's commands, living lives that would be examples for all to follow.

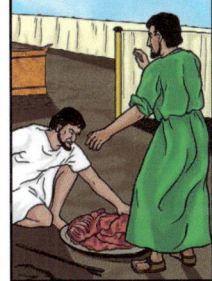

Show Illustration #2

Instead of following God's commandments, Hophni and Phinehas were disobedient and full of wickedness. For example, when the Jewish people brought animal sacrifices to the house of God, Hophni and Phinehas wanted the best part of each animal for food for themselves. God allowed priests to use a part of most sacrifices. Hophni and Phinehas, however, were not satisfied. They wanted more. So they had their servant take what they wanted. If the people reminded the servant that the offerings belonged to God, he snatched by force what Hophni and Phinehas wanted.

Stealing what belonged to God was only one of the sins of these wicked priests. They openly did other evil deeds which God had forbidden; and they influenced some of the people to sin, too.

Now Eli knew about his sons' wickedness and he spoke to them about it. "Why do you do such things?" he asked. "You are making the people sin. And you, yourselves, are sinning against the Lord."

Hophni and Phinehas ignored their father and went right on doing the same evil deeds. And Eli let them continue serving as priests in the tent of the Lord.

One day a man of God came to Eli with a warning, saying, "Listen carefully, Eli. This is what the Lord says to you: 'Long ago I, the Lord, chose your father and his children to be My priests–to offer sacrifices to Me, and to wear the ephod [the priest's special garment of honor]. You have fattened yourselves on the sacrifices and offerings which belonged to Me. You have honored your sons more than you have honored Me. You have allowed them to continue as priests while they lived in wickedness. Because of this, none of your family will live to old age. Your two sons, Hophni and Phinehas, will both die on the same day. And I shall choose a new priest who will do what I want him to do.'"

What a dreadful message of condemnation!

3. GOD CHOOSES SAMUEL FOR HIS SERVICE
1 Samuel 3:1-21

Through all those sad days, young Samuel faithfully followed God's way. He had been set apart for God before he was born. Remembering that, helped him to live a holy life.

Show Illustration #3

One night when Eli and Samuel lay asleep, a voice called, "Samuel!"

Samuel, thinking it was Eli who had called, ran to him and said, "Here I am, for you called me."

But Eli replied, "I didn't call you. Lie down again."

Had Samuel been dreaming? Perhaps the wind had made a sighing sound like a voice. But, there! He heard it again: "Samuel!"

Samuel ran again to Eli saying, "Here I am. You *did* call me."

"No, I didn't call you, my son. Lie down again."

A third time it happened. Then Eli understood the Lord was calling Samuel. So he said, "Lie down, Samuel. And when He calls say, 'Speak, Lord, for Your servant is listening.'"

Samuel lay down as he was told. Again the Lord called, "Samuel! Samuel!" Immediately Samuel answered, "Speak, for Your servant is listening."

Then the Lord told Samuel events which would happen in the future. "I shall severely punish Eli and his family because his sons have sinned and he did not discipline them," God said.

The next morning Samuel went about his usual duties in the tent of the Lord. He felt unhappy, as he thought of the punishment which God would send to Eli and his sons.

When Eli said, "Tell me what the Lord said to you," Samuel told him everything. So Eli replied, "He is the Lord. May He do what seems good to Him."

Eli knew God would act in fairness. He must judge and condemn those who sin willfully. Eli and his sons had been set apart by God for His service. Instead, they did as they pleased. Now it was too late. The choice had been made.

In the days which followed, Samuel with determination served God faithfully. And the Lord was with him. Soon everyone knew that God had cosen Samuel to be His prophet.

4. ELI AND HIS SONS ARE JUDGED BY GOD
1 Samuel 4:1-18

Later, Eli's two sons were killed in battle, both on the same day–just as God had foretold.

Show Illustration #4A

When news of their death reached Eli, he fell off his official chair (at the gate of the tabernacle), broke his neck, and died. Because he had allowed his sons to continue in their sinful ways, none of his family ever again was chosen to serve the Lord God.

Show Illustration #4B

Samuel, however, continued in the work of the Lord, faithfully serving the One for whose service he had been set apart.

God wants us to serve Him, too. Will *you* serve Him this week? Exactly what do you think He wants you to do?

(*Teacher:* Encourage born-again class members to discuss how they can serve the Lord *this week.*)

Lesson 2
GOD'S HOUSE IS SANCTIFIED

NOTE TO THE TEACHER

Samuel was a *person* who was set apart for God even before he was born, as we learned in our last lesson. Today we learn that *things* too may be set apart for God. In this case, it was the house of God that was sanctified.

For about 400 years the house of God was a tent enclosed with curtains. (In English, it is called a tabernacle.) God's children moved from one place to another and it was necessary that they have a movable place of worship. Much later, in the time of Hezekiah, the house of God was a magnificent temple–beautiful and very costly.

The tent and the temple where God met with His people were important to Him as well as to His people. He had given careful instructions for building them. (See Exodus 25:1–27:21; 1 Chronicles 22:1-19; 28:1–29:9; 2 Chronicles 2:1–5:14.)

More important than knowing exactly what God's tent and temple looked like is knowing that God sanctified them. Each was a holy place. For a person to treat God's house or anything connected with it in an unholy way meant certain death. (See, for example, Leviticus 10:1-3; Numbers 16; 1 Chronicles 13:9-10.) Ahaz (of our lesson) destroyed the furnishings and closed the doors of God's sanctified house. And he was punished. Hezekiah restored the furnishings and opened the doors and called the people back to the worship of the holy, living God. And as a result, Hezekiah was blessed by God.

Begin the lesson by asking students to tell how they have served God since the last session.

Scripture to be studied: 2 Chronicles 28:1-4, 16-27; 2 Kings 18:1-7; 2 Chronicles 29:1–31:2; Romans 6:1-23.

The *aim* of the lesson: To show that things, as well as people, may be set apart for the Lord.

What your students should *know:* Believers are to yield to God, not allowing themselves to be ruled by sin.

What your students should *feel:* A desire to live lives that are set apart for God.

What your students should *do:* Ask God to forgive their sin and yield obediently to Him.

Lesson outline (for the teacher's and students' notebooks):

1. God's people worship idols, ignoring the house of God (2 Chronicles 28:1-4, 16-27).
2. King Hezekiah orders the people to set apart themselves and the house of God (2 Kings 18:1-7; 2 Chronicles 29:1-19).
3. King Hezekiah leads the people in sanctifying themselves for God (2 Chronicles 29:20–30:13).
4. The people prove they are set apart by getting rid of sinful practices (2 Chronicles 30:14–31:2; Romans 6:1-23).

The verse to be memorized:

Ye are washed . . . ye are sanctified . . . ye are justified in the name of the Lord Jesus, and by the Spirit of our God.
(1 Corinthians 6:11b)

THE LESSON

To be sanctified is to be set apart for God. When Paul wrote his letter to the Romans, he knew that sometimes they would find it hard to keep their lives pure. He knew that Satan would try to make them do wrong. And that is equally as true today. Satan is never pleased when we choose to obey God instead of obeying him. He (Satan) continually tempts us to sin.

Because the Lord Jesus died and took the punishment for our sins, each of us is to count that our old sinful self is dead. We are to turn our backs on sin. As Christ rose again from the dead, we are to live a new life in Him. Just as God declares us righteous because of Christ, so He counts us sanctified–set apart for His use.

1. GOD'S PEOPLE WORSHIP IDOLS, IGNORING THE HOUSE OF GOD
2 Chronicles 28:1-4, 16-27

Hundreds of years before Paul wrote his letter to the Romans, God's sanctified people were living sinful lives. This is what happened:

Show Illustration #5

Ahaz, the king of Judah, did not love God. He led his people deep into sin during the 16 years of his reign. God had said that His people should not worship idols or images (see Exodus 34:17; Leviticus 19:4). Yet King Ahaz made images of Baalim and worshiped them. God had forbidden His people to worship the heathen god Moloch (see Leviticus 18:21). Even so the king himself disobeyed God's Word and built altars to Moloch and sacrificed some of his own children on those altars. Throughout the whole land the wicked king built altars, burned incense and offered sacrifices to idols.

Because God was displeased with Ahaz's great wickedness, He allowed enemies to come into the land and capture many of the people as prisoners. Do you think this caused Ahaz to turn back to God and ask forgiveness for his sins? No. Instead, he turned to the king of a neighboring country, Assyria, and asked for his help. But this only added to his trouble because he had to pay large sums of money and send many gifts to the Assyrian king–who took his gifts but did not help him.

Trouble piled upon trouble, and things grew worse for King Ahaz. But instead of turning to God, he sinned even more. He said, "Because the gods of my enemies have helped them win against me, I will sacrifice to *those* gods." So he built more altars and sacrificed to more false gods.

Not only did Ahaz worship false gods, but he forbade his people to worship the true God of Heaven. He destroyed much of the furniture in the house of God and closed its doors. So God's temple stood empty and silent, while throughout the land, king and people bowed before idols.

2. KING HEZEKIAH ORDERS THE PEOPLE TO SET APART THEMSELVES AND THE HOUSE OF GOD
2 Kings 18:1-7; 2 Chronicles 29:1-19

Then one day Ahaz died, and his 25 year old son, Hezekiah, became king of Judah. The young king was not at all like his wicked father. Hezekiah loved and served the true God of Heaven. He knew that God would help him lead his people in the right way. There was much to be done. His nation was in ruin because of his father's sins.

Show Illustration #6

As soon as Hezekiah became king, he opened the doors of God's house–the doors which his father had closed. Then he called those whose duty it was to care for the temple. The king spoke sternly, "Hear me! Sanctify yourselves and sanctify the house of the Lord God of your fathers, and carry the filthiness out of the holy place. Our fathers sinned and turned their backs against God. They stopped worshiping God and turned to the worship of idols. Because of this sin, the wrath of God came upon them. But now the Lord has chosen you to stand before Him and serve Him."

Did you hear that? King Hezekiah told his people to *sanctify* God's house–set it apart once more for the worship of God. They were to regard it as a holy place and keep it free from sin for the glory of God. They were also to sanctify themselves–separate themselves from sin, and keep themselves pure for the service of God.

The caretakers of God's house listened carefully. They knew that King Hezekiah's words were true. So they obeyed and made themselves fit for the Lord's service. Then they set to work sanctifying the house of the Lord–repairing and cleaning it.

When the task was finished, they reported to the king: "We have finished cleaning the house of the Lord. We have repaired the broken altar and furniture. We found and restored the objects which Ahaz had thrown away. All is sanctified and ready for worship once more."

3. HEZEKIAH LEADS THE PEOPLE IN SANCTIFYING THEMSELVES FOR GOD
2 Chronicles 29:20–30:13

Show Illustration #7

Early the next morning, King Hezekiah summoned the rulers of the city and led them to God's house. There king and people together presented sacrifices as an offering for their sins. While the sacrifice was being offered on the altar, the singers sang, the trumpeters played and the people worshiped God. What a glad day! The people returned to the Lord and asked forgiveness for their sins. The temple was clean and set apart once again for the worship of God. Joyfully they sang praises to God.

So great was their joy that they planned a celebration. They remembered that many years before, God's people had celebrated the Passover, to bring to mind one of the many miracles which God had performed for them in the wilderness. Now it had been a long time since the feast had been celebrated. Hezekiah and his people wanted to remember again the marvels God had done for them in the past.

Hezekiah sent letters throughout all his kingdom and to the other Jewish tribes inviting them to share in the Passover celebration. He said, "Come and ask God to forgive your sins just as we have done. God is kind and loving and will not turn away from you if you return to Him." Hezekiah wanted others to know the joy he and his people now knew since they had set themselves apart for God. "Yield yourselves to the Lord and enter into His house which He has sanctified forever. Serve the Lord your God," Hezekiah urged.

Swiftly the king's messengers carried his invitation to all the Jewish tribes. Some laughed and mocked and continued in sin. But a great number of people accepted Hezekiah's invitation and came to the capital city of Jerusalem to share in the feast.

4. THE PEOPLE PROVE THEY ARE SET APART BY GETTING RID OF SINFUL PRACTICES
2 Chronicles 30:14–31:2; Romans 6:1-23

Show Illustration #8

Together they tore down the altars of the false gods which Ahaz had built in Jerusalem. Then they feasted and worshiped God together, and the king prayed, saying, "The good Lord pardon every one who prepares his heart to seek God." God heard Hezekiah's prayer and forgave the people. For seven days the feasting continued, with praying and singing praises to God. The people had such a glad time that they decided to continue for seven *more* days.

When the days of feasting and rejoicing had ended, the people went together into the other cities in the land of Judah and destroyed all the idols that remained from the days of King Ahaz. They broke the images in pieces, cut down the groves of trees where the idol worship had been performed and completely destroyed the altars to the false gods. Then all the people of God returned to their own cities.

It was a wonderful time as king, people and servants of God sanctified themselves for the worship of the Lord.

Years later Paul commanded the Roman believers to do the same thing. And God wants us to live sanctified lives, too. Paul told them and us: "Count yourselves to be dead indeed unto sin, but alive unto God through Jesus Christ our Lord. Do not let sin rule your body, that you should obey its sinful desires. And do not yield yourselves to the devil for his purposes. But put yourselves in God's hands for His purposes." (See Romans 6:11-13.)

If you have truly placed your trust in the Lord Jesus Christ, God has announced you righteous. He says, too, you are sanctified. Have you sanctified–set apart–yourself for God's holy purpose? If, instead, you have been yielding to sin, right now is the time to ask God to forgive you and to purpose with His help to live the life of a set-apart person.

Lesson 3
DANIEL SANCTIFIES HIMSELF

NOTE TO THE TEACHER

All of salvation–including sanctification–is the gift of God. God has provided sanctification by: (1) the precious blood of the Lord Jesus Christ and (2) the indwelling Holy Spirit. The person who places his trust in Christ as Lord and Saviour is sanctified immediately. That is, he belongs to God because of his new birth and is therefore set apart by Him for His purpose. Thereafter, throughout the believer's entire lifetime, it will be his responsibility to keep unbroken his fellowship with the Lord.

In the life of Daniel we see the triumph of one who purposed in his heart to serve the Lord faithfully. Help your scholars to see that this may be their experience. Encourage those who have not faithfully set themselves apart for God by showing that Paul sometimes had a similar experience. But help them to see the urgency of confessing their sin (1 John 1:9) and determining, with God's help, to serve Him instead of surrendering to the old fleshly nature.

Scripture to be studied: Daniel 1 and 6; Romans 7

The *aim* of the lesson: To teach the believer's responsibility to keep himself set apart for God.

What your students should *know*: God has set apart for Himself those who believe in the Lord Jesus Christ as Saviour.

What your students should *feel*: Responsible to keep themselves from sin.

What your students should *do*: Ask God to help them keep themselves from sin.

Lesson outline (for the teacher's and students' notebooks):

1. God's set-apart people are responsible to set themselves apart for Him (Romans 7:15-25; Daniel 1:1-7).
2. God blesses Daniel because he sets himself apart (Daniel 1:8-20).
3. Daniel's sanctification is tested (Daniel 6:1-17).
4. God honors Daniel (Daniel 6:18-28).

The verse to be memorized:

Ye are washed . . . ye are sanctified . . . ye are justified in the name of the Lord Jesus, and by the Spirit of our God.
(1 Corinthians 6:11b)

REVIEW

What does it mean to be sanctified? *(To be set apart for God)* You will remember that in Old Testament times, priests were sanctified for the work of the Lord. Some of them lived pure lives which pleased God. Others lived only to please themselves and satisfy their own desires. Do you remember the names of two of the wicked priests whom God had to condemn for their sins? *(Hophni and Phinehas)* Was Ahaz a good king? *(No)* What did he do? *(He built altars to false gods and worshiped idols. He also destroyed the furniture of the house of God and closed its doors.)* What did good King Hezekiah do? *(He tore down the altars to idols. He restored God's house and led the people again to worship the true and living God of Heaven.)*

THE LESSON

1. GOD'S SET-APART PEOPLE ARE RESPONSIBLE TO SET APART THEMSELVES FOR HIM
Romans 7:15-25; Daniel 1:1-7

When we receive Christ as our Saviour, God sanctifies us. It is then our responsibility to obey God's will and keep our lives clean for His use. If we have sinful thoughts and do sinful deeds, we displease God and are not useful to Him. We ourselves are wretched. (See Romans 7:24.)

The Apostle Paul had had this experience and wrote about it in his letter to the Romans. Like all believers, Paul was sanctified the moment he was born again. From then on there were two natures inside him. The old nature, which was his from the day he was born, caused him to want his own way. It was his will against God's will. His new nature, which he received at the time of his new birth, desired to do God's will. So his two natures fought against each other.

Show Illustration #9A

At times Paul chose to do God's will (Romans 7:22). Whenever this was so, the Holy Spirit controlled him and the Lord Jesus Christ shone out of his life.

Show Illustration #9B

At other times, Paul followed his own will. He hated to do so, nevertheless he did. (See Romans 7:15, 19.) The Holy Spirit still lived within him. But instead of the glory of the Lord Jesus shining out of Paul, all that showed was Paul's old sinful nature.

Like Paul, we sometimes let our old natures control us. But the person who lives a normal Christian life is one who honors God. If we determine with His help to live for Him and follow His way, He gives us power to overcome sin.

Daniel lived long before the Apostle Paul. He was young when he determined to keep himself pure for God's service. Let me tell you about him:

Daniel was born in the land of Judah many years after good King Hezekiah had died. The king who ruled Judah in Daniel's time did not love and serve God, as Hezekiah had done. Instead, he was wicked like King Ahaz. So God caused His people to be punished by their enemies exactly as He had warned them. (See 2 Kings 20:16-19; Isaiah 39:6-8.)

Mighty armies came from the land of Babylon, fighting and killing many of God's people. The land was again in ruins and some of the finest young men were taken captive. (See 2 Chronicles 36:4-8; 2 Kings 24:1-5.)

One of the young prisoners, Daniel (see Ezra 8:1-2), had a keen mind and a strong body. He and some of his friends were chosen by King Nebuchadnezzar of Babylon to serve in his royal palace. These healthy, intelligent young men would be useful to the king.

Nebuchadnezzar knew that Daniel and his friends loved and served God. Even their names spoke of God. Daniel's name meant "God is my judge." The names of his friends meant "God is gracious", "Who is what God is?" and "God has helped". Their names reminded the young men of the one true God to whom they belonged.

The king wanted his prisoners to worship the gods of Babylon, so he commanded that their names be changed. He named Daniel, Belteshazzar which means "Keeper of the hidden treasure of Bel". Bel was the sun god, the most important of the Babylonian idols. Daniel's friends were also given names to remind them of gods made by human hands. Do you suppose their new names caused them to forget the true and living God? No, indeed! Their *names* were changed; their *hearts* were not. They remained faithful to the God of Heaven.

2. GOD BLESSES DANIEL BECAUSE HE SETS HIMSELF APART
Daniel 1:8-20

King Nebuchadnezzar gave orders: "Daniel and his friends are to be treated well. They are to live comfortably. Teach them the language, laws and customs of Babylon."

Nebuchadnezzar commanded: "Feed the young men the finest meat from the king's own table. Serve them the king's wine."

Now the prisoners faced a hard test. Daniel knew it would be wrong to eat the king's meat. He, Daniel, served the true and living God. The king worshiped false gods–and doubtless the meat had been offered to idols. Daniel would have nothing to do with idolatry and had determined in his heart not to defile himself. Also, God had said His people were not to drink wine. (See Deuteronomy 28:39; Proverbs 20:1; 23:29-30.) Daniel had set himself apart for God, and he would not spoil himself with sin.

Daniel belonged to God and wanted to please Him. He did not want to do anything sinful. He knew that the food and wine would soon lead him to other ungodly Babylonian customs.

Show Illustration #10

Daniel told the king's servant, "I can't eat the king's meat and drink his wine. Let me have vegetables to eat and water to drink."

The servant was afraid. "If you and your friends don't look as healthy as the other young men in the palace," he began, "the king will be angry with me. He may behead me!"

Daniel answered, "Give us a trial of ten days. Allow us to eat the food for which we have asked. Then compare us with the others who eat the king's food. If we do not look better than they, you decide what to do with us."

The servant agreed. At the end of ten days, Daniel and his friends looked much healthier than those who had eaten the king's meat and drunk his wine. So the servant allowed them to continue eating only vegetables and water. God was pleased with these four and gave them great wisdom and skill.

Indeed, when King Nebuchadnezzar questioned Daniel and his friends, he found them to be ten times wiser than all the wisest men in his kingdom!

Even though Daniel lived in an ungodly country, he remembered that because he belonged to God he was set apart for God. As new kings came to the throne in Babylon, Daniel helped each one, doing his work wisely and well. So God caused him to become exceedingly important in the king's government.

3. DANIEL'S SANCTIFICATION IS TESTED
Daniel 6:1-17

One day King Darius named Daniel to be the head over all the princes and rulers of his kingdom. The princes were jealous and watched Daniel carefully, hoping he would do something wrong which they could report to the king.

But Daniel lived a pure life and did his work faithfully. They could not find fault with him. "We will not be able to find anything wrong with him, unless it concerns the law of his God," they said. Then they had an idea.

The princes went to King Darius. "O King, live forever!" they began. "We princes have decided this law should be made: Whoever makes a request from any god or any man except you, O King, should be thrown into the den of lions."

The king liked what he heard and immediately signed the law. The law could not be changed or broken, because the king himself had signed it.

What would Daniel do? If he were seen praying to God, he would be thrown to the lions. Do you think he was afraid? Which was more important to him–his life or God?

Show Illustration #11

"Daniel has broken the law!" they shouted. "Throw him to the lions!"

The king was angry with himself for having made such a law. But the princes reminded him, "Your law cannot be changed, O King."

All day long the king worried, trying to think of a way to save Daniel. But he could not. His law was unchangeable.

Again the princes went to the king. Sadly he ordered, "Give Daniel to the lions." To Daniel he said, "Your God, whom you serve continually, will save you." Even though the king worshiped idols, he knew that Daniel believed in the true and living God who could save him from hungry lions.

Daniel was hurled to the lions. A rock securely closed the opening and the king sealed the den with his own seal.

4. GOD HONORS DANIEL
Daniel 6:18-28

That night the king could not sleep. Early the next morning he hurried to the den. "O Daniel, servant of the living God!" he called. "Is your God able to deliver you from the lions?" From the depths of the den, Daniel's voice echoed, "O King, God has sent His angel and shut the lions' mouths, so they have not hurt me."

Show Illustration #12

The all-powerful God of Heaven had performed a miracle. Daniel was alive and unharmed because he believed in God. The king was delighted. But he was angry with the princes who had persuaded him to make the law. So he sent for them, their children and their wives, and ordered *them* to be cast into the lions' den. Before they fell to the bottom of the den, they were broken in pieces by the vicious beasts.

When King Darius saw how God had protected Daniel, he sent a message to the people of his kingdom. "Everyone must worship the God of Daniel. He is the living God," the king declared.

Will you be like Daniel? Daniel determined that he would not defile himself, and God helped him to remain pure. If God has washed you in the precious blood of the Lord Jesus Christ, He has forgiven your sins and set you apart for Himself. Will you determine, with His help, to keep yourself from sin–set apart for God?

Lesson 4
BELIEVERS ARE TO LIVE SANCTIFIED LIVES

NOTE TO THE TEACHER

Three times in the Bible, believers in Christ are spoken of as Christians. But 62 times they are called saints. It will be a great help to us personally, if we think of ourselves and fellow believers as saints . . . holy . . . sanctified. We are set apart by God for His purpose.

The three subjects taught in the first eight chapters of Romans are referred to in chapter eight. It reads: "There is therefore now no *condemnation* to those who belong to Christ Jesus." In verse 34 Paul writes, "Who will *condemn* us? Will Christ? No! For He is the One who died for us and rose for us and is sitting next to God in Heaven praying for us."

Paul also writes, "Who would dare to accuse us, whom God has chosen for His own? Would God, the Judge of all the earth, do that–when He has *justified* us?" (See 8:33.) In 8:26-27, Paul speaks of the Holy Spirit who prays for the *saints*.

Condemnation, justification, sanctification. These three subjects are taught in the first eight chapters of Romans. Chapter eight closes with a tremendous promise: All believers are more than conquerors through Christ. And because of Him, nothing or no one can ever separate us from Him. God, the righteous One, keeps His own. Wonderful, glorious truth!

Scripture to be studied: Romans 5:12–8:39

The *aim* of the lesson: To show how a believer sanctifies (sets apart) himself for God.

What your students should *know*: Those who are washed in the blood of the Lord Jesus Christ are sanctified by God and should separate themselves from sin.

What your students should *feel*: Determined to live set-apart lives that will honor God.

What your students should *do*: Ask God to help them live holy lives.

Lesson outline (for the teacher's and students' notebooks):

1. Believers are set apart for God, like the Most Holy Place in God's house.
2. Believers sanctify themselves by following God's way willingly.
3. Believers are sanctified by God's Word and prayer.
4. Believers will one day be perfect like the Lord Jesus.

The verse to be memorized:

Ye are washed . . . ye are sanctified . . . ye are justified in the name of the Lord Jesus, and by the Spirit of our God.
(1 Corinthians 6:11b)

THE LESSON

We have already learned that when we receive the Lord Jesus Christ as our Saviour, we are justified–that is, we are declared righteous by God. At the same time we are sanctified. To be sanctified is to be set apart for God.

1. BELIEVERS ARE SET APART FOR GOD, LIKE THE MOST HOLY PLACE IN GOD'S HOUSE

Show Illustration #13

In the days of Samuel and for hundreds of years before that time, God's people worshiped Him at a tent. It was no ordinary tent, but a special one built exactly as God had commanded–one which could be carried from place to place. One part of the tent was known as the Holy Place. Most of the religious ceremonies were performed there. A smaller section of the tent was veiled from view. It was known as the Most Holy Place *or* the Holy of Holies. The high priest alone was allowed to go into the Most Holy Place–and only on special occasions. It was in the Most Holy Place that God met with His people. Just as its name suggests, it was a sanctified place. It was set apart for God by God Himself. He gave careful instructions as to the use and care of His tent. If any person disregarded His instructions, that person was immediately struck dead. (See Leviticus 10:1-2; Numbers 16:1-50; 2 Samuel 6:3-7.) This is how holy God's tent was.

Today God does not dwell in a tent or temple. Instead, He lives in His born-again children. (See 1 Corinthians 6:19-20; 2 Corinthians 6:16-18.) It will help us to live as we should if we remind ourselves constantly, "I am God's temple. He lives in me."

Does this mean that we are now perfect and will never again do anything wrong? Oh, no! (See 1 John 2:1-2.) As long as we live on earth we shall have sinful natures. We shall sin. Our memory verse (which is from the Letter which Paul wrote to the believers in Corinth) says, "You are sanctified, you are justified." He called the Corinthian believers saints (1 Corinthians 1:2). But he also scolded them for their many faults. He wrote, "I speak to your shame . . . you do wrong!" (See 1 Corinthians 5:1-2; 6:1-8.) They were not perfect.

Nor are we perfect. But the moment we place our trust in the crucified, resurrected Son of God, we are set apart by God for Himself. Because He lives in us, we are holy. We are sanctified. We are saints. (Remember, please, that each word has the same meaning: *to be set apart for God*.) Paul also addressed the Romans as saints. (See Romans 1:7.) They and we are saints because we are members of the family of God. And this never changes. Just as you were born into your parents' family and will always be the child of your parents, so, when you are born into the family of God, you are His child forever. You are a saint. Never forget it!

An earthly father usually sets certain standards for his children. He expects each member of his family to live up to his own reputation. Children who love their father are eager to obey him and want to live to honor him. So it is in God's family. His loving children whom He has sanctified are eager to live lives that prove they are sanctified. Samuel was set apart for God even before he was born. For him, serving the Lord meant that when he was a young child he had to leave his family in order to do God's work. All his life he continued to live wholly for God.

Daniel, a prisoner in a foreign land, had to live among people who worshiped false gods. But he set himself apart for the true and living God. He behaved as a sanctified child of God. Samuel and Daniel were not sanctified because they tried to live good lives. They wanted to live good lives because they were sanctified.

So it is with us. We become saints by receiving the Saviour. We do not do good to become saints. Because we are saints, we try to do good. Our lives should match what God says we are: sanctified, holy (1 Peter 1:15-16). How can this be? How can we keep our lives pure and separate from sin? How can we live lives that are set apart for God? There are several ways. Here are a few to be listed in your notebook, please:

2. BELIEVERS SANCTIFY THEMSELVES BY FOLLOWING GOD'S WAY WILLINGLY

Show Illustration #14

Like Daniel, we must determine not to sin nor do anything which will lead us to sin. (Daniel refused the king's meat and wine.) God has given us a *will*—the ability to make choices. We can choose to do one thing and refuse to do another. God does not make our choices for us. But He does give us the ability to make right choices.

Let us look in our Bibles to see what the great Apostle Paul wrote to the Roman Christians (which is for us, too, you know). (*Teacher:* Read Romans 6:11-13 and encourage group discussion. With Ephesians 4:23–5:15, let students choose areas of their own lives which need attention and list them in their notebooks.)

God begs you to present your body, a living sacrifice, holy (sanctified, *set apart*), acceptable to Him, who is your reasonable service. (See Romans 12:1-2.) When you determine to keep yourself from sin and do the will of God, you are sanctifying yourself.

3. BELIEVERS ARE SANCTIFIED BY GOD'S WORD AND PRAYER

Show Illustration #15A

In Samuel's days it was not unusual for God to speak personally to His own. Now, since the Word of God is printed in the Bible, God speaks to us through it. He has set down certain principles which help us to know what is right and what is wrong. As we study it and obey it, we are sanctified.

When the Lord Jesus was here on earth, He told His disciples, "You are made clean by the words I have spoken to you." (See John 15:3.) Later, when He was praying to God the Father, He said, "Make them holy for Yourself by the truth. Your Word is truth." (See John 17:17.) Years after that, the Apostle Paul told the Ephesian believers that they were sanctified by the Lord Jesus and made clean through the Word of God. (See Ephesians 5:26.) If we are to follow God's way, we must know His Word, the Bible. And we must live according to what it says (1 Peter 3:15).

As we have seen, we set ourselves apart for God (1) when we are willing to do His will and (2) when we study His Word and obey it.

Show Illustration #15B

It would have been easy for Daniel to have followed the crowd in obeying the rulers of the land where he was a prisoner. He might have worshiped their idols. Did he do that? He certainly did not. He did something far more difficult. He prayed faithfully to God–the God in whom his captors did not believe. He did it, even though he knew he would be thrown to the lions. But God honors those who honor Him. He kept Daniel safe.

Like Daniel, we who are God's "set apart" children, must set apart time each day to talk with our Heavenly Father, so that we may please Him. Often in our prayer time God shows us how we have displeased Him. We must confess that sin to Him–name the sin, ask forgiveness and promise Him that with His help, we shall not do such sins again. (See 1 John 1:9.) If we are to please God, we must hate sin as He hates it.

Although we who belong to God are not yet perfect, we should try each day to be more like Him. Because He has set us apart as His own, we should *will* to obey Him, learn *His Word* and talk with Him in *prayer*. Then we shall be able to resist temptation and to separate ourselves from sin.

4. BELIEVERS WILL ONE DAY BE PERFECT LIKE THE LORD JESUS

Show Illustration #16

One glad day when we see the Lord Jesus, we shall be changed. Our old sinful natures will be gone forever and we shall be perfect–as perfect as the Lord Jesus. Think of that!

The Bible tells us that here and now we are God's children. But when we see the Lord Jesus, we shall be *like Him*. It is this hope that helps us to keep ourselves pure, for we know how pure Christ is. (See 1 John 3:1-4.)

Are you looking forward to seeing the Lord Jesus? Are you walking God's way, separating yourself from sin? Are you keeping your life pure for His glory? Will you determine, right now, with God's help, to live a sanctified life? Remember, you are washed in the precious blood of the Lord Jesus Christ. You are sanctified in God's sight. He has said so. Your part is to live personally as one who has already been set apart by God. Since God *has* sanctified you, will you choose to live a holy life?

www.ingramcontent.com/pod-product-compliance
Lightning Source LLC
Chambersburg PA
CBHW060807090426
42736CB00002B/189